THE DRESS

<u>Titles Available from Forty-Two Books</u>

Peaks of Madness: A Collection of Utah Horror

Satan Speaks! Contemporary Satanic Voices

Putrescent Poems Volume 1

Strange Stories Volume 1

<u>Forthcoming in 2020</u>

They Walk Among U s: A Collection of Utah Horror

All Titles Available on Amazon.com or from Forty-Two Books

THE DRESS

A POETIC RESPONSE

Daniel Cureton

42
Books
Salt Lake City

A Poetic Response to 2015's

"The Dress" debate:

Color and Fashion.

THIS PAGE IS BLACK AND BLUE

THIS PAGE IS WHITE AND GOLD

<u>BIBLIOGRAPHY</u>

Grant, Kate. "The Dress: Roman Originals Co-Founder Peter Christodoulou on How Viral Image Left Company Sitting Pretty." *Independent*, 30 Oct. 2015, https://www.indepen dent.co.uk/news/uk/home-news/the-dress-roman-originals -co-founder-peter-christodoulou-says-viral-image-leaves- company-sitting-a6715786.html. Accessed 24 Jan. 2020.

Swiked. "Guys Please Help Me—". Whoa wow wow!, 15 Feb. 2015. *Internet Archive Wayback Machine*, 27 Feb. 2015, https://web.archive.org/web/20150227014959/ http://swiked.tumblr.com/post/112073818575/guys-please -help-me-is-this-dress-white-and. Accessed 24 Jan. 2020.

References

Shenton, Zoe. "Who is Swiked? Girl Goes Viral After Scottish Singer Posts Dress Picture." *Mirror*, 27 Feb. 2015, https://www.mirror.co.uk/3am/celebrity-news/who- swiked-girl-goes-viral-5241813. Accessed 24 Jan. 2020.

About the Author

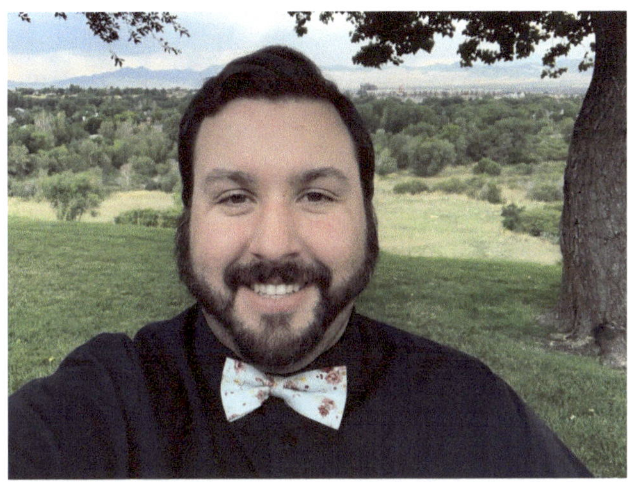

Daniel is a writer, editor, publisher, and avant-garde poet. His poetry exposes the deeper meanings of experiential living and his stories are idea platforms. He holds an MA in English from Weber State University.

He is currently working on several publication due out in 2020 including: *They Walk Among Us: A Collection of Utah Horror, Putrescent Poems Volume 2*, and *Utter Filth!*, his next book of poems.

Originally from South Carolina, Daniel currently lives in Salt Lake City, UT with his cat Oliver, a cross eyed Siamese.

9 781734 006773